Wee Bites & Nibbles

Wee Bites & Nibbles

Manners and menus for the tiniest tea drinkers

Jennifer Stowe
Three Sisters' Tea Room

To Julia - my VBF!

Mum

For families that want to introduce children to the delights and graces of afternoon tea customs, Jennifer Stowe has done all the planning for you in *Wee Bites and Nibbles*, providing themed teas with recipes, activities and tips on tea service and etiquette. I applaud her for setting out to help our children love the beauty of the afternoon tea ritual. Her creative tea party plans should do just that!

– Angela Renals
Destinationtea.com

I have made wonderful memories with my daughters while partaking in tea at Three Sisters' Tea Room. *Wee Bites and Nibbles* allows us to continue making memories at home while recreating the delicious recipes and fostering a love of all things beautiful. Not only is this book full of culinary delights but it inspires me to slow down and enjoy what matters most, my children. It is simply beautiful.

– Tiffany Boyd
Three Sisters' Tearoom Patron

Contents

Welcome to the world of *Wee Teas*!
Let ***Giggles*** be your hostess as you read about each
tea and help you decide which one to host for your
guests first. Sometimes a friendly face is nice to
see within the pages of a book, and that's just what
Giggles is, a friendly face!

"A Thing of Beauty is a Joy Forever..."

... so John Keats once wrote. We couldn't agree more! Tea is a thing of beauty, so is friendship and manners and because of this, from time to time our tearoom hosts what we call, *Wee Teas*. These unique afternoon teas, designed especially for our youngest guests, are offered in hopes of instilling a love, not just of tea but, of all *beautiful* things. We believe manners matter and that social graces never go out of style. Friendships are essential and quiet moments spent with loved ones nurture our souls. Indeed these are *beautiful* things!

We do our best to create an elegant tearoom environment that is distinctly set apart from everyday life, yet our teas are **real**. **Real**, wholesome food is served on **real** china with **real** linens. The table settings are visually attractive and truly make our guests feel special and ensure they will be on their best behavior. Yes, it is a tea party but not a sugar-laden, child-focused, free-for-all. Our young guests are future adults after all and these *Wee Teas* are their training ground!

So when considering how to spend an afternoon with the children in your life, you could choose to do many things. We encourage you to choose what is **real** and *beautiful* and plan to host one of these delightful, delicious, tried and true *Wee Teas*.

19

Thank goodness for tea! What would the world do without tea? How did it exist? I am glad I was not born before tea.

– Sydney Smith

Summer

A Pretty Purse
Tea

Tea Brewing
Times and Temperatures

Everyone has their own taste preferences, but here are some good guidelines to follow when making tea for your guests:

Types of Tea	Length of Time	Temperature of Water
White	2-3 minutes	170°
Green	2-3 minutes	180°
Oolong	3-4 minutes	185°
Black	4-5 minutes	boiling
Rooibos	5-8 minutes	boiling
Herbals	7-8 minutes	190°

Tea too weak? Add more tea to the pot not more steeping time.

What girl, no matter her age, does not love a Pretty Purse?

Maybe girls are simply born with a purse-loving gene or maybe it is a learned affinity, either way, this charming Wee Tea will be enjoyed by all who attend.

What to do:

 Invite each guest, even the moms attending, to bring their favorite purse to the tea. Go around the table and ask each guest to share the meaning behind their purse and why it is their favorite. You are sure to enjoy the stories!

 Serve tea to your guests.

 Read a few picture books to the wee guests about purses while they eat. Some titles for you to consider might include:

The Purse
    by Kathy Caple
My Granny's Purse
    by P. H. Hanson
Lilly's Purple Plastic Purse
    by Kevin Henkes
What's in Your Purse
    by Abigail Samoun
The Lady with the Alligator Purse
    illustrated by Nadine Westcott

Check your local library for these and many other fun titles connected to this topic. Read each story out loud a few times prior to the tea to familiarize yourself with the stories and to work out your dramatic flare.

 Instruct and assist your wee guests with the purse craft. Each guest can make their own pretty paper plate purse with lots of decorative embellishments. Then take the girls outside for a nature walk and find a few interesting items to put in their purses such as; a pine cone, a feather, a wild flower, a piece of lichen, etc.

 Moms enjoy the same menu as their daughters at their own table.

The Menu

Sweets

Pretty Purse Butter Cookies

Make one batch of the butter cookie recipe and using a purse-shaped cookie cutter, (easily found online) cut out one large cookie for each guest. Frost and decorate using sprinkles. You could let your guests decorate a pre-baked cookie in place of the paper plate purse craft as the activity for this tea.

Ingredients
- 2 cups all-purpose flour
- 1/2 teaspoon baking powder

- 1/2 teaspoon salt
- 1 1/2 sticks (3/4 cup) unsalted butter, softened
- 1 cup sugar
- 1 large egg
- 1/2 teaspoon vanilla

Instructions

Preheat oven to 375°F.

Whisk together flour, baking powder, and salt in a small bowl.

Beat together butter and sugar in a large bowl with an electric mixer at medium-high speed until pale and fluffy, about three minutes. Beat in egg and vanilla. Reduce speed to low, then add flour mixture and mix until just combined. Form dough into a ball and cover with a piece of plastic wrap. Chill dough until firm, at least four hours. Flour the counter and roll out a piece of the dough to 1/4 inch thick. Using purse-shaped cookie cutter, cut out the cookies and place on a parchment-lined cookie sheet, arranging cookies about 1 inch apart. Bake cookies until edges are golden, 12 to 15 minutes. Cool on racks completely.

Frost cooled cookies with white frosting and cover with sprinkles.

Makes about two dozen cookies.

Savories

BCT Tea Sandwiches

Have one sandwich for each guest.

Ingredients
- one 8oz package of cream cheese
- black pepper to taste
- bunch of fresh basil
- tomatoes
- one 8oz package of cheddar cheese, sliced
- loaf of bread such as Pepperidge Farm's Very Thin White

Instructions
Spread two slices of thin white bread with softened cream cheese mixed with a little black pepper then add basil leaf, cheese and tomato slice on one of the bread slices and top with the other. Trim crusts and cut sandwich into two triangles, three fingers or four squares and arrange attractively on tea tray.

 Scones

Lemon-Raspberry Scones

One batch makes approximately 12 scones. Have one for each guest.

Ingredients
- 2 cups all purpose flour

- 2 Tablespoons sugar
- 2 Tablespoons baking powder
- ½ teaspoon salt
- 4 Tablespoons unsalted butter cut into pieces
- 1 Tablespoon lemon peel, grated
- 2 eggs, beaten
- ½ cup buttermilk
- ½ cup fresh or frozen raspberries

Instructions

Preheat oven to 425 degrees F.

In a large bowl, mix together the flour, sugar, baking powder, and salt. Add butter pieces and cut into flour mixture with pastry cutter. Butter should be the size of peas. Add grated lemon peel. In another bowl mix together eggs and buttermilk and then raspberries. Add wet ingredients to dry ingredients until moistened. Let batter rest about five minutes. Pat down on floured board to ½ inch thickness. Cut into triangles or circles or hearts using cookie cutters and place on parchment-lined cookie sheet. Bake about 12 minutes until lightly golden. Serve warm with fresh cream.

Easy Fresh Cream

Ingredients
- 1 cup heavy whipping cream, whipped
- 1 cup sour cream
- 1/4 cup powdered sugar

Instructions

Mix heavy whipping cream with sour cream and powdered sugar. Cover with plastic wrap and let sit on counter for six hours. Stir and then place in refrigerator until ready to serve, at least four hours.

Tea

Celestial Seasoning's Raspberry Zinger

This tea is good hot, warm, cool or cold and just perfect for this tea! Lightly sweeten with raw sugar, if desired, and serve in pretty tea cups.

Punch

Pink Lemonade Punch

Mix one container of frozen pink lemonade concentrate with two liters of sparkling water, add ice and garnish with fresh raspberries and serve in a large glass punch bowl. Very refreshing!

How to Make a Paper Plate Purse

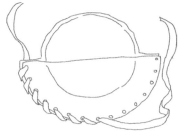

- Fold two paper plates in half.
- Cut one plate in half along fold line.
- Trim ruffled rim off the other plate, starting at fold line on left side, ending at fold line on right.
- Lay half plate on top of other plate creating a pocket between the two plates.
- Punch holes through both plates along edge about 1" apart.
- Cut one yard of 1/4" ribbon and thread through holes. Tie the ends together creating a shoulder strap.
- Embellish as desired!

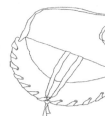

Autumn

Molly's Pilgrim Tea

Cambric Tea

In Edwardian nurseries, children were given a delicious and gentle brew of very weak tea blended with milk and sugar in hopes of giving them health and vitality and to help them feel grown up during tea time. This delicate drink was also served to soothe an upset tummy and was given to the elderly for this same reason.

Cambric tea got its name from the beautiful Cambric fabric made in the textile town of Cambria, France. Cambric fabric was soft and creamy-white, much like the tea. Sadly, while cambric tea was a very popular beverage during the late 19th and early 20th centuries, it is virtually unknown today. Revive this forgotten beverage by serving it at your next wee tea!

We have all had a moment when we feel we do not fit in.

Maybe it happened when we moved to a new town or started a new school or job. It's hard and can be very lonely. Well, just like the English Pilgrims of the 17th Century, many "modern" pilgrims have moved to this country seeking to make America home and that is just what Molly's family did in the book, *Molly's Pilgrim*. This is an excellent tea to host close to Thanksgiving and every wee guest will be cheering for Molly as this story ends.

What to do:

 Invite each guest to dress in warm autumn attire in the splendid colors of the season.

 Serve tea to guests.

 Read the book, *Molly's Pilgrim* by Barbara Cohen. Practice reading this book a few times before the tea.

There are several foreign words and phrases which might leave you tongue-tied if you are not prepared.

 Instruct and assist wee guests with corn husk doll craft. All guests should make their dolls step by step together and then embellish them to their liking by adding aprons, hair, eyes, baskets, brooms, etc.

 Moms enjoy the same menu as their daughters at their own tables.

The Menu

 Sweets

Chocolate Dipped Dried Apricots

Plan to have at least two for each guest.

Ingredients
- 30 dried apricots
- 1 cup semi-sweet chocolate chips

Instructions
Purchase a bag of dried apricots. Melt about 1 cup of semi-sweet choco-

late chips in a glass bowl in the microwave or in a double boiler on the stove top. When chocolate is melted and very smooth, dip half of each apricot into the melted chocolate. Place on a parchment-lined cookie sheet to harden. Repeat with remaining apricots.

 Savories

Mini-Cheese Balls with Assorted Crackers

Ingredients
- one 8oz package cream cheese
- 8oz cheddar cheese, shredded
- 1/2 teaspoon black pepper
- 1/2 teaspoon dried rosemary
- assorted crackers

Instructions
Mix softened cream cheese with shredded cheddar cheese, rosemary and black pepper. Roll mixture into 1 inch balls and arrange on a pretty plate with assorted crackers. Have at least one ball for each guest.

 Scones

Nutmeg Scones

One batch makes approximately 12 scones. Have one for each guest.

Ingredients
- 2 cups all purpose flour
- 2 Tablespoons sugar

- 2 Tablespoons baking powder
- ½ teaspoon salt
- 1 teaspoon ground nutmeg
- 4 Tablespoons unsalted butter cut into pieces
- 2 eggs, beaten
- ½ cup heavy cream

Instructions

Preheat oven to 425 degrees F.

In a large bowl, mix together the flour, sugar, baking powder, salt and nutmeg. Add butter pieces and cut into flour mixture with pastry cutter. Butter should be the size of peas. In another bowl mix together eggs and heavy cream. Add wet ingredients to dry ingredients until moistened. Let batter rest about five minutes. Pat down on floured board to ½ inch thickness. Cut into triangles or circles or hearts using cookie cutters and place on parchment-lined cookie sheet. Bake about 12 minutes until lightly golden. Serve warm with honey butter.

Honey Butter

Mix one stick of softened butter with 1 teaspoon cinnamon, 1/4 cup honey and 1/4 cup powdered sugar until very smooth and creamy. Serve in a cut glass bowl with warm nutmeg scones.

 Tea

Celestial Seasoning's Cinnamon and Apple Spice

Serve hot with a cinnamon stick in each tea cup.

Orange Cider Punch

Mix 16 ounces orange juice with 1 container of frozen apple juice concentrate and 2 liters of sparkling water in a glass punch bowl. Add ice and garnish with fresh orange slices.

How to Make Cornhusk Dolls

Soak corn husks in warm water for 20 minutes before beginning craft

- Lay 8 corn husks together. Tie approximately 1" from narrow end of husks with yarn. Trim to even out top edges.

- Fold four corn husks over tied area and tie again approximately 1" from top, this forms the head.

- Roll 1 corn husk and tie each end with yarn about 1/2" from ends.

- Separate bottom husks of skirt in half and insert the smaller corn husk roll.

- Tie underneath the roll to create the arms.

- To get doll to stand, trim skirt ends. If necessary, re-wet doll's skirt and fluff into bell shape.

- Faces and hair are not traditional but can certainly be added!

"Do you want your adventure now, or would you like to have your tea first?" asked Peter.

– J. M. Barrie
The Adventures of Peter Pan

Winter

Fairy Ballerina
Tea

How to Brew a Perfect Pot of Tea

- *boil a kettle of fresh spring water*
- *place one heaping tablespoon of loose tea or two tea bags into a small tea pot*
- *add boiled water to tea pot and let steep for 4-5 minutes if black and 7-8 minutes if herbal*
- *using a tea strainer, pour tea into a tea cup for you and your guest*
- *sweeten to taste, add milk and enjoy with a good friend*

The perfect tea for the start of a new year is...

A *winter-white-fairy-ballerina-dream-come-true* tea! This is just the afternoon event sure to warm up the chilliest January day! With a young ballet teacher to lead the girls in a simple floor routine, each guest will surely feel like the Sugar Plum Fairy by the time she leaves the party.

What to do:

Invite all your young guests to come to the tea dressed as fairies or ballerinas.

If you do not know a young ballet teacher, contact a local dance studio and ask if any student might be well-suited to come to your ballerina tea. Discuss details thoroughly with her, including payment. Ask her to come dressed in a beautiful white tutu with a sparkling crown and teach the girls the basic ballet arm and feet positions and then a lovely curtsey. Allow the girls plenty of practice time while playing Tchaikovsky's, *Nutcracker Suite.*

When the little fairies have had enough of dancing, seat them and serve tea.

While your guests are enjoying a refreshing tea, read them a story about a young ballerina. A particular favorite for this theme is *Angelina Ballerina* by Katharine

Story by Katharine Holabird   Illustrations by Helen Craig

Holabird. This volume tells a sweet story about an aspiring ballerina who must learn self-control and restraint. Both the story and illustrations are gentle and charming.

 After tea, allow time for each guest to have her picture taken, in pose, with the fairy ballerina. You might even create an attractive backdrop just for this purpose.

 Moms enjoy the same menu as their daughters with a sandwich substitute.

The Menu

Sweets

Gingersnap Ballerina Cookies

This is an old European recipe which explains the unique measurements. Have two for each guest, depending on the size of your cutter.

Ingredients

- 6 ounces butter
- 16 ounces sugar
- 2 eggs
- 4.7 ounces molasses
- 2 teaspoon white vinegar
- 1 lb. 3 ounces all purpose flour
- 1 1/2 teaspoon baking soda
- 1 Tablespoon ginger powder
- 1/2 teaspoon cinnamon powder

Instructions

Preheat oven 325 degrees F

Cream butter and sugar until light, add eggs and mix well. Add molasses and vinegar, mixing well. Sift together flour, baking soda, ginger and cinnamon. Add the dry ingredients to wet and mix until well blended. Chill dough. Roll out dough onto a floured counter top and cut out ballerinas using a ballerina-shaped cookie cutter, easily found online. Place on a baking sheet lined with parchment paper. Bake 10-12 minutes, until golden and crisp. When completely cooled, decorate with melted white chocolate or frosting.

Clementine slices

Have 3-4 for each guest

...dipped half way in melted chocolate. Delicious!

Girls' Peanut Butter and Jam Flower
Sandwiches

Ingredients

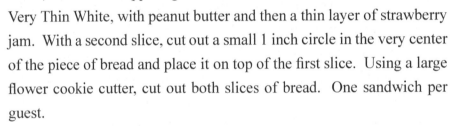

- peanut butter
- strawberry jam
- loaf of white bread

Instructions

Spread one piece of thin white
bread, such as Pepperidge Farm's
Very Thin White, with peanut butter and then a thin layer of strawberry
jam. With a second slice, cut out a small 1 inch circle in the very center
of the piece of bread and place it on top of the first slice. Using a large
flower cookie cutter, cut out both slices of bread. One sandwich per
guest.

Moms' Cream Cheese and Canadian Bacon
Sandwich

Ingredients

- one 8oz package cream cheese
- 1/2 teaspoon powdered garlic
- 1 teaspoon chopped chives
- loaf of white bread
- round slices of Canadian bacon

Instructions

Mix chopped chives and powdered garlic into softened cream cheese. Set aside. Using a large 3 inch circular cookie cutter and very thin white bread, such as Pepperidge Farm's Very Thin White, cut out two circles. Spread a generous amount of filling on one of the circles and top with a slice of Canadian bacon. Leave as open face sandwiches or top with a second slice of bread. One sandwich per guest.

 Scones

Lavender White Chocolate Scones

One batch makes 12 scones. Have one scone for each guest.

Ingredients

- 2 cups all purpose flour
- 2 Tablespoons sugar
- 2 Tablespoons baking powder
- ½ teaspoon salt
- 4 Tablespoons unsalted butter cut into pieces
- 1 Tablespoon chopped culinary lavender
- 2 eggs, beaten
- ½ cup half and half
- ½ cup coarsely chopped white chocolate chips

Instructions

Preheat oven to 425 degrees F.

In a large bowl, mix together the flour, sugar, baking powder, and salt. Add butter pieces and cut into flour mixture with pastry cutter. Butter should be the size of peas. Add chopped lavender and white chocolate chips. In another bowl mix together eggs and half and half. Add wet ingredients to dry ingredients until moistened. Let batter rest about five minutes. Pat down on floured board to ½ inch thickness. Cut into triangles or circles or hearts using cookie cutters and place on parchment-lined cookie sheet. Bake about 12 minutes until lightly golden. Serve warm with lavender-infused butter.

Lavender-Infused Butter

Cream one stick of soften, unsalted butter with 1 teaspoon chopped lavender buds, cover with plastic wrap and allow to sit on counter for 6 hours then refrigerate until ready to use.

Tea

Organic India Tulsi Sweet Rose Herbal

Sweeten tea with honey, if desired and serve hot.

Punch

Raspberry Lemonade

Despite the chill outside the dancers may still need a cool drink to refresh them after dancing.

Mix one container of frozen raspberry lemonade concentrate with two liters of sparkling water in a large punch bowl. Add ice and garnish with a few frozen raspberries or lemon slices.

Spring

The Empty Pot
Tea

Tea Time

Do:

- Wash hands before coming to the table
- Wait for hostess to be seated before beginning to eat
- Say grace
- Place napkin on lap
- Thank cook for a delicious meal

Don't:

- Use electronic devices at the table
- Wear a ball cap to the table
- Grab for items out of your reach
- Speak with food in your mouth
- Wipe mouth on sleeve
- Leave the table without asking to be excused

As the days lengthen and the breeze is fresh with the smells of spring...

...the perfect time has come for an Empty Pot Tea.

This is a fine tea to share with the wee gentlemen on your guest list. With a nice mixture of boys and girls at your gathering, it is a perfect occasion to review basic table manners, such as; what to do with one's napkin, which utensil to use when, how to pass the sugar down the table, and the proper method of boys seating the girls. Ask the children to role play these techniques and maybe even demonstrate some unacceptable table manners for the other guests to correct!

What to do:

Invite all guests to come dressed appropriately to tea. You set the standard and state it clearly in the invitation. Dresses, jackets and ties, etc.

Review table etiquette. Have fun learning together through roll playing and skits.

Serve guests tea and allow them to put into practice the manners they have just learned.

While guests are eating, read the excellent character-building book titled, *The Empty Pot* by Demi. In this old Chinese fable, a young boy is confronted with a choice regarding honesty. The ending is sure to please all your guests and will challenge them to always do their best.

After tea and the story have conclude, instruct guests in the craft. Move to a pre-staged table containing small terra cotta pots and saucers, a small bowl of pea-sized gravel, a large bowl of potting soil, plenty of plastic spoons, and a watering can. Allow guests to prepare a pot for a seed. Once the children have prepared their pots, give each child one great big dried lima bean seed to plant and water. As they tend the seed at home and watch it grow, encourage them to remember that Ping chose honesty and so should they!

Moms enjoy the same Spring-inspired menu as the children at their own tables.

The Menu

Sweets

Dirt Dessert

Have one cup for each guest

Spoon homemade or purchased chocolate pudding into small, clear, plastic cups, then top with ground Oreos and garnish with a fresh sprig of mint. Refrigerate until ready to serve.

Savories

Chive Cream Cheese and Spouts
Tea Sandwiches

One sandwich per guest

Ingredients

*   one 8oz package of cream cheese
*   fresh chives
*   white bread
*   sprouts

Instructions

Thoroughly blend
cream cheese with
1 tablespoon finely
chopped fresh chives and
spread on thin bread, such as Pepperidge Farm's Very Thin White. Cut
into 2 inch rounds or triangles. Top with a generous mound of sprouts.
Serve as closed or open-face sandwiches on a tea tray. Alternatively,
trim bread crusts off a full slice of bread, spread cream cheese, add
sprouts then roll up slice of bread diagonally, starting at one corner.
Cut in half and tie a long thin chive around the center of each half.
Stand sandwiches upright on flat end. A mixture of both would make a
very charming presentation.

Scones

Mini-Chocolate Chip and Mint Scones with Fresh Whipped Cream

Makes 12 scones. Have one scone for each guest.

Ingredients

- 2 cups all purpose flour
- 2 Tablespoons sugar
- 2 Tablespoons baking powder
- ½ teaspoon salt
- 4 Tablespoons unsalted butter cut into pieces
- 1 Tablespoon finely chopped fresh mint or 1/2 teaspoon mint extract
- 2 eggs, beaten
- ½ cup half and half
- ½ cup mini-chocolate chips

Instructions

Preheat oven to 425 degrees F.

In a large bowl, mix together the flour, sugar, baking powder, and salt. Add butter pieces and cut into flour mixture with pastry cutter. Butter should be the size of peas. Add chopped mint or mint extract and mini-chocolate chips. In another bowl mix together eggs and half and half. Add wet ingredients to dry ingredients until moistened. Let batter rest about five minutes. Pat down on floured board to ½ inch thickness. Cut into triangles or circles or hearts using cookie cutters and place on parchment-lined cookie sheet. Bake about 12 minutes until lightly golden. Serve warm with fresh whipped cream.

Tea

Jasmine Green Tea

Both Numi and Twinings are brands that carry this type of tea and are easily found in most grocery stores. Serve hot and sweeten with honey, if desired.

Punch

Refreshing Limeade Punch
As refreshing as Springtime!

Mix one container of frozen limeade concentrate with two liters of soda water in a large punch bowl. Add ice and garnish with a few lime slices.

"I don't feel much like Pooh today,"
said Pooh.
"Then let us have tea until you feel like
Pooh again,"
replied Piglet.

- A. A. Milne

Winnie the Pooh

Summer

The Dot
Tea

A Proper Tea Time Place Setting

In order for guests to express good manners, they must be provided with the proper tools! A proper tea time place setting is essential, yet simple, as you can see above.

Sometimes all we need is someone to believe in us...

...and then we're inspired to achieve great things! Most young children love to draw and paint yet sadly by the time they get to school many think they cannot draw. Such is the case with Vashti in *The DOT* until someone encourages her to just make a mark. Now she's off encouraging her friends to do the same.

Choose a warm summer day for this tea. Invite both girls and boys of all ages and after tea and story time, let your guests make their dot in a pre-staged outdoor art studio. You just might discover a Renoir or Picasso in your group!

What to do:

- Invite guests to wear colorful, comfortable clothing that can get paint-stained or to bring a smock.

- Serve tea to your guests and read them the picture book titled, *The DOT* by Peter Reynolds. This is a very short book so spend a little time discussing the *en plein air** painting method

the Impressionist painters so heartily embraced in the late 19th century in France. Tell them they will get to try it out themselves right after tea!

Instruct and assist guests in the craft. Give each child a pre-made artist's pallet and a paint brush. Here's a very clever pallet made of recycled materials. Fill each cap with primary colors of tempra paint. Next lead children outside where an easel has been

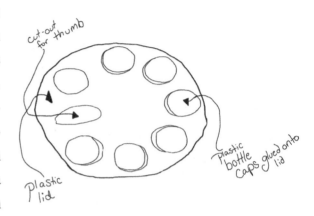

made for each of them using three tall sticks tied together at the top and arrange into a teepee. Hammer small nails into two of the sticks, at the same height, to create a shelf on which to place the child's canvas, a large sheet of water color paper taped onto a piece of foam board. Encourage everyone to make their DOT and don't forget to have them sign it!

Moms enjoy the same menu at their own table but pesto *DOT* sandwiches are substituted for peanut butter and jelly.

* During the late 19th century, when the impressionist movement was in full swing in France, artists preferred painting out of doors

to capture the moment in time or moments of early morning light. This became extremely popular and soon artists everywhere were painting in fresh air, or en plein air.

The Menu

DOT Sugar Cookies

Make one batch of sugar cookies and using round cookie cutters of various sizes, cut out cookies. Frost cookies in different colors by mixing small amounts of purchased or homemade frosting with different colors of liquid food coloring. Sprinkle top of frosted cookies with sparkling dusting sugar. Plan on 2-3 cookies per guest, depending on size.

Ingredients
- 2 cups all-purpose flour
- 1/2 teaspoon baking powder
- 1/2 teaspoon salt
- 1 1/2 sticks (3/4 cup) unsalted butter, softened
- 1 cup sugar
- 1 large egg
- 1/2 teaspoon vanilla

Instructions
Preheat oven to 375 degrees F.

Whisk together flour, baking powder, and salt in a small bowl.

Beat together butter and sugar in a large bowl with an electric mixer at medium-high speed until pale and fluffy, about three minutes. Beat in egg and vanilla. Reduce speed to low, then add flour mixture and mix until just combined. Form dough into a ball and cover with a piece of plastic wrap. Chill dough until firm, at least four hours.

Flour the counter and roll out a piece of the dough to 1/4" thick. Using round cookie cutters, cut out the cookies and place on a parchment-lined cookie sheet. Bake cookies until edges are golden, 12 to 15 minutes. Cool on racks completely. Frost cooled cookies and sprinkle with sugar. Makes about four dozen cookies

Savories

Peanut Butter and Jelly DOT Sandwiches

One sandwich for each guest.

Using a large round cookie cutter, cut out rounds of soft white bread. On half of the rounds, cut out a much smaller circle in the center. Spread the whole round with peanut butter then jelly. Next place the round with the cut out on top of the jelly. Using strawberry jelly makes a nice red DOT in the center of the sandwich but any type of jelly will work well.

Follow same instructions for moms' sandwiches but substitute home-made or pre-packaged pesto, instead of peanut butter and jelly, for sandwich filling.

Scones

Rainbow Scones

One batch makes approximately 12 scones. Have one for each guest.

Ingredients

- 2 cups all purpose flour
- 2 Tablespoons sugar
- 2 Tablespoons baking powder
- ½ teaspoon salt
- 1 Tablespoon rainbow colored sprinkles
- 4 Tablespoons unsalted butter cut into pieces
- 2 eggs, beaten
- ½ cup heavy cream

Instructions

Preheat oven to 425 degrees F.

In a large bowl, mix together the flour, sugar, baking powder, salt and sprinkles. Add butter pieces and cut into flour mixture with pastry cutter. Butter should be the size of peas. In another bowl mix together eggs and cream. Add wet ingredients to dry ingredients until moistened. Let batter rest about five minutes. Pat down on floured board to ½ inch thickness. Cut into 2 inch circles using a cookie cutter and place on parchment-lined cookie sheet. Bake about 12 minutes until lightly golden. Serve warm with butter.

Lemon Iced Tea Punch

This lovely beverage is your tea and punch all in one! Enjoy in tall glasses, or even wine glasses!

To 6 black teabags add 1/2 gallon of boiling water and 1/4 cup of sugar or honey. Stir well and let steep for 8 minutes. Remove teabags and chill in refrigerate until ready to serve. To serve, pour cold tea into punch bowl. Add one liter of sparkling water, one container frozen lemonade concentrate, plenty of ice and several round slices of oranges, lemons and limes.

If you are cold, tea will warm you.
If you are too heated, it will cool you.
If you are depressed, tea will cheer you.
If you are excited, it will calm you.

— *Gladstone*

Summer

A Nancy Drew *Tea*

Tea Tray Line Up

Be sure to assemble your three-tiered tray in the right order. Guests eat from

the bottom up!

Top Tier- Sweets
mini-muffins, truffles, cookies,
fudge, fruit, etc.

Middle Tier- Scones
and spreads such as whipped
cream, lemon curd, jam and butter

Bottom Tier- Savories
finger sandwiches, mini-quiches,
vegetable wraps, etc.

Every female can recall her years of infatuation with the girl-sleuth... Nancy Drew.

Often the "tween" years mark the time of greatest admiration for the girl who could tap dance, golf, speak French, down hill ski, gourmet cook, and grow award-winning flowers while setting fashion trends, driving an adorable, powder blue convertible and solving one mystery after another. What young girl wouldn't be impressed?!

This tea is just right for young girls between eight and twelve but don't be surprised if Mom or Grandmother come to tea just as enthusiastic as your young guests!

What to do

Invite guests to dress as Nancy might have during any one of the decades her books were being written and revised. (1930s-1970s are the most fun.)

Serve tea to your guests while two young girls act out a short Nancy Drew skit.*

Allow mothers and daughters plenty of time for pleasant conversation during tea.

Following tea, hand each guest a quiz** and pen. Working alone, encourage them to answer all the Nancy Drew trivia questions they can in five minutes. Review quiz together and award copies of Nancy Drew books to those with the highest scores. Have fun!

The Menu

"Togo" Terrier Cookies

These adorable dog-shaped cookies are named in honor of Nancy's beloved fox terrier, Togo. Depending on size of cookie cutter, have one to two cookies per guest.

Ingredients

- 1 cup butter
- 1 cup sugar
- 2 eggs
- 2 Tablespoons milk
- 1/2 teaspoon baking powder
- 2 1/2 cups quick oats
- 2 1/2 cups flour

Instructions

Cream butter and sugar until light. Add eggs and continue mixing until well incorporated. Beat in oats. Stir baking powder into flour and add to butter and sugar mixture. Add enough milk to make a pliable dough. Roll out dough into a wide rectangle. Wrap rectangle in plastic and refrigerate for about twenty minutes. Remove from refrigerator and allow dough to soften before rolling out to 1/4 inch thick on a lightly floured surface. Using dog-shaped cookie cutter, cut out cookies and bake at

375 degrees F for 10 to 12 minutes. Cool on wire racks. Decorate as desired.

River Heights Melon Salad

The name of Nancy's fictitious hometown is River Heights which inspired the name for this fruit salad. Serve a small bowl to each guest.

Ingredients
* Grated rind and juice of 2 limes
* 1/4 cup honey or sugar
* mint sprigs (optional)
* 1 watermelon cut into bite sized pieces
* 2 cantaloupes cut into bite sized pieces
* 1 bunch grapes washed and stemmed

Instructions
Whisk together lime rind, juice, and honey. Place fruit in a large bowl and pour lime dressing over it. Mix well. Leave at room temperature for 30 minutes. Refrigerate before serving. Serve in cut glass bowls or tea cups.

 Savories

Ned's Favorite Club Sandwiches

Ned was sweet on Nancy and as a result spent a lot of time with her investigating mysteries. Ned was well-know for his love of sandwiches and this is one sure to please him…and your guests. Plan of two sand-

wich squares per guest (half of a whole sandwich).

Ingredients

- sliced white or wheat bread
- butter
- deli-sliced turkey
- sliced munster or provolone cheese
- lettuce
- tomato, sliced

Instructions

Select a thin white bread, such as Pepperidge Farm's Very Thin White or Wheat for this sandwich. With three slices of bread assemble as follows: spread butter on bottom slice of bread. Top with deli-sliced turkey and munster or provolone cheese. Add a second slice of bread on top of turkey and cheese and top that with a piece of lettuce and a slice of tomato. Butter a third slice of bread and lay atop the vegetables. Cut into four square pieces. Pierce each square with a decorative toothpick to keep sandwich together, if desired.

 Scones

Blueberry Scones

In the Mystery of the Tolling Bell, Nancy and her friends stop at a tearoom and are served some warm blueberry scones much like these you can make for your guests. One batch makes 12 scones. Have one scone per guest.

Ingredients

- 2 cups all purpose flour
- 2 Tablespoons sugar
- 2 Tablespoons baking powder
- ½ teaspoon salt
- 1/2 cup fresh or frozen blueberries
- 4 Tablespoons unsalted butter cut into pieces
- 2 eggs, beaten
- ½ cup heavy cream

Instructions

Preheat oven to 425 degrees F.

In a large bowl, mix together the flour, sugar, baking powder, and salt. Add butter pieces and cut into flour mixture with pastry cutter. Butter should be the size of peas. Gently toss in blueberries and coat with flour/butter mixture. In another bowl mix together eggs and cream. Add wet ingredients to dry ingredients until moistened. Let batter rest about five minutes. Pat down on floured board to ½ inch thickness. Cut into 2 inch circles using a cookie cutter and place on parchment-lined cookie sheet. Bake about 12 minutes until lightly golden. Serve warm with butter.

 Tea

English Breakfast Tea
with cream and sugar

This classic tea is the perfect choice for a gal like Nancy. Select a good quality brand such as, Twinings or Harney and Sons and enjoy with plenty of cream and sugar.

Punch

Mixed Berry Punch

Into a large punch bowl, mix one container mixed berry or fruit punch frozen concentrate with two liters of sparkling water, add ice and garnish with fresh berries.

* Nancy Drew Tea Skit

Helen: Hi Nancy! Can I come in?

Nancy: Oh, hi Helen! How are you?

Helen: I'm fine. Very fine. I just had to stop over to see you --
looking at tables of girls
Oh, I see you already have company. Hello everyone. I hope I'm not interrupting.

Nancy: No, no of course not. We were just having some tea.

Helen: Tea? Excellent! I brought some blueberry scones. Remember last week when we visited that quaint little tea room while solving the mystery of the Tolling Bell?

Nancy: Oh yes! They were utterly scrumptious! Did the owner give you the recipe?

Helen: She did indeed and here is my first attempt at making them myself.

Nancy: *Wistfully*
That was a fun day. We solved the mystery and you got engaged to Bob. He's such a swell guy. You two will be very happy together. May I see the ring?

Helen: Of course! It's right here --
hysterical
Oh -- what -- my -- where? My ring! It's gone! Oh, Nancy where can it

be? I just had it. It's a mystery and you must help me solve it.

Nancy: Okay, calm down Helen. Take a deep breath. Tell me the last time you remember having the ring.

Helen: *Looking worried but calm*
Well, I had it at breakfast and then I took it off to make the scones. I set it on the window sill -- Oh, but you know what? In the middle of mixing them up the milkman came to the kitchen door. He wanted to be paid. I had to get Mother from the study to come take care of that. He could have taken the ring from the window sill.

Nancy: Who's your milkman?

Helen: *Embarrassed*
Ernie.

Nancy: Ernie? Ernie? He's been delivering our milk since we were babies. We've known him all our lives. No he could not be the thief. Did anyone else come by this morning?

Helen: *Thinking*
Yes, a telegram was delivered for Dad. The man came to the front door but followed me into the back hall where I found him change for a tip. He left through the kitchen door. He could have been --
getting confident
Yes, I'm sure he is the thief. He had little beady eyes and a shifty way of looking around the house.

Nancy: Okay good. Now we're getting somewhere. What did he look like?

Helen: *Getting excited using hand gestures*

Well, he was short, but taller than me and his hair was dark, but not as dark as mine and he had a mustache ... I think ... or maybe it was glasses...

Nancy: *Getting frustrated*

Oh, bother! I know. Let's share the scones with our guests and see if a little tea will shed any light on this mystery.

Helen: *Deflated*

Oh -- alright. Here you go. I hope you enjoy them They'd better be good. They should be good. Especially with butter and some of that jam on them.
Turns to Nancy
Oh Nancy, will we ever find my engagement ring?

Rachel: Uh, Nancy? Helen? I think I've solved the mystery and found your ring.

Nancy and Helen: You have?

Rachel: Yes. It's right here in the middle of my scone. Clearly it must have fallen into the batter and been baked in. See?
Holds ring up for all to see. Helen runs to grab ring and hugs Rachel.

Helen: Thank you! Thank you!

Nancy: Well it looks like we've just solved another mystery right here in River Heights.

** Nancy Drew Quiz

- What was the name of Nancy's fictitious home town?

- What was Nancy's age when the books debuted in 1930?

- What was the book title of the first Nancy Drew Mystery?

- What was Nancy's little dog's name?

- Who are Bess and George?

- Who is Nancy Drew's housekeeper?

- Where is Nancy Drew's mother?

- What name does Nancy use as an alias in one of her mysteries?

- Who is Ned Nickerson?

- Where does he go to college?

- What is the color of Nancy's hair?

- What is the occupation of Carson Drew, Nancy's father?

- What did Dad give Nancy as a birthday gift when she turned 16?

Answers
1. River Heights
2. sixteen
3. The Secret of the Old Clock
4. Togo
5. Nancy's cousin (Bess) and friend (George).
6. Hannah Crumb
7. she died when Nancy was three years old
8. she uses many different names
9. Nancy's boyfriend
10. River Heights University
11. Titian blond
12. he is a lawyer
13. a maroon roadster

Steps for Hosting a Perfect Tea Party

1. Pick your *date and time*.

2. Send out the *invitations*; be sure to state:
    *   date
    *   time
    *   dress
    *   how and when to RSVP

3. Choose the *theme* including decor, colors, and activities.

4. Plan the *menu*; select your:
    *   sweets
    *   scone
    *   savories
    *   soup
    *   tea
    *   punch

5. Once all RSVPs have been received arrange your *seating plan.* To ensure that all of your guests have an enjoyable time, be sure to introduce everyone as they are seated. Don't leave anyone out.

6. On the *day of the tea*: Assemble your sandwiches. Place

on trays covered with damp paper towel and plastic wrap. Refrigerate until tea time. Next, mix up the scones. Bake just before guests arrive. Just before it's tea time, make punch and start to boil water. Lay out all food on three-tiered trays. Items such as cookies, chocolate-dipped dried fruit, and cheese balls can be made a few days ahead of time, kept in the fridge and brought out the day of the tea.

May you always have walls for the winds, a roof for the rain, tea beside the fire, laughter to cheer you; those you love near you, and all your heart might desire.

- *Irish Blessing*

Resource Page

Books

All book titles mentioned in this book can be found at
www.amazon.com

Teas

Celestial Seasonings
www.celestialseasonings.com
4600 Sleepytime Drive
Boulder, CO 80301
855-972-0539
Email: celestialseasonings@worldpantry.com
Easily found in most grocery stores

Organic India USA
www.us.organicindia.com
7088 Winchester Circle, Suite 100
Boulder, CO 80301
888-550-8332
Found in health food stores or online

Numi Tea
www.numitea.com
866-972-6879
Numi Organic Tea Headquarters
P.O. Box 20420
Oakland, CA 94620

Twinings' Tea
www.twiningsusa.com
800-803-6695
Twining North America, INC
Consumer Service
777 Passaic Ave., Suite 230
Clifton, NJ 07012

Food

Pepperidge Farm Very Thin White or Wheat Bread
www.pepperidgefarm.com
595 Westport Ave
Norwalk, CT 06851
1-888-737-7374
Found in most grocery stores

Corn Husks
Found in Mexican markets, some grocery stores or online at
www.amazon.com
Corn Husks Hojas para Tamal-Maley by Mama Maley
$10.99 per pound includes s&h

Cookie Cutters

Purse-Shaped Cookie Cutter
www.amazon.com
1 Piece Biscuit Cookie Cutter Handbag Purse Metal Jelly Gingerbread
Molds by Cookie Cutter
$3.13 + shipping

Flower-Shaped Cookie Cutter
www.amazon.com
Scalloped Edge / Flower Cookie Cutter - 3.8 Inches - US Tin Plated
Steel by Ann Clark Cookie Cutters
$5.99 includes s&h

Ballerina-Shaped Cookie Cutter
www.amazon.com
Pretty Ballerina Girl Cookie Cutter by The Fussy Pup
$14.79 includes s&h

Dog-Shaped Cookie Cutter
www.amazon.com
Labrador Dog Cookie Cutter - 4.25 Inches - Tin Plated Steel by Ann
Clark Cookie Cutters
$5.99 includes s&h

Coloring Pages

Permission granted by author to copy coloring pages for
personal use connected to this book.

Suggested Uses:
Activities at *Wee Teas*
Placemats at *Wee Teas*
Wee Tea take home gifts
Place cards at *Wee Teas*

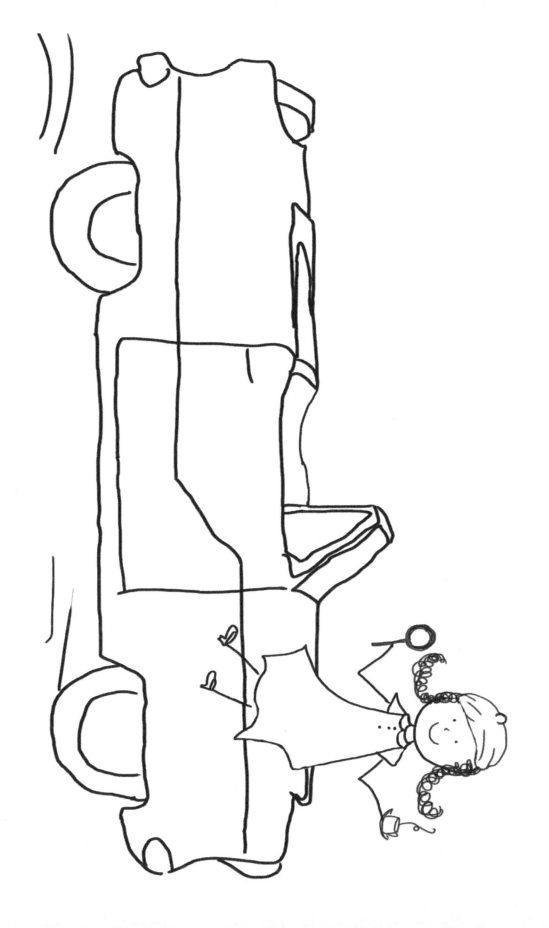

Made in the USA
Middletown, DE
03 February 2021